The INSIDE GUIDE

FAMOUS NATIVE AMERICANS

Sitting Bull

By Simon Pierce

Cavendish Square

Published in 2025 by Cavendish Square Publishing, LLC
2544 Clinton Street Buffalo, NY 14224

First Edition

Website: cavendishsq.com

Library of Congress Cataloging-in-Publication Data

Names: Pierce, Simon, author.
Title: Sitting Bull / Simon Pierce.
Description: Buffalo, NY : Cavendish Square Publishing, [2025] | Series:
Inside guide: Famous Native Americans | Includes index.
Identifiers: LCCN 2024002988 | ISBN 9781502671073 (library binding) | ISBN
9781502671066 (paperback) | ISBN 9781502671080 (ebook)
Subjects: LCSH: Sitting Bull, 1831-1890–Juvenile fiction. | Hunkpapa
Indians–Biography–Juvenile literature.
Classification: LCC E99.H795 P54 2025 | DDC 978.004/9752440092
[B]–dc23/eng/20240215
LC record available at https://lccn.loc.gov/2024002988

Editor: Jennifer Lombardo
Copyeditor: Jill Keppeler
Designer: Deanna Lepovich

The photographs in this book are used by permission and through the courtesy of: Cover, pp. 14, 18, 28 (left) Courtesy of the Library of Congress; p. 4 Adam Outdoors Photography/Shutterstock.com; p. 6 Indian Counting Coup MET page9/Wikimedia Commons; pp. 7, 10, 15, 16, 20, 24 Everett Collection/Shutterstock.com; p. 8 Pan-American Exposition - A Glimpse at the Indian Congress/ Wikimedia Commons; p. 12 Bozeman Trail, the forts and the Indian territories/Wikimedia Commons; p. 22 Tibbut Archive/Alamy Stock Photo; p. 26 BC Images/Shutterstock.com; p. 28 (right) Vicki L. Miller/Shutterstock.com; p. 29 (left) Andrea Izzotti/Shutterstock.com; p. 29 (right) Luciano Mortula - LGM/Shutterstock.com.

CPSIA compliance information: Batch #CSCSQ25: For further information contact Cavendish Square Publishing LLC at 1-877-980-4450.

Printed in the United States of America

CONTENTS

Sitting Bull was born near where the Grand River meets the Missouri River, which is shown here.

JUMPING BADGER

Chapter One

Sitting Bull was born around 1831 in what is now the state of South Dakota. His parents gave him the name "Jumping Badger." He was part of the Hunkpapa band of the Lakota. The Lakota are divided into groups. They have adopted the name "Sioux" as a collective term, but they prefer to be called by their individual group's name. The groups all speak the same language but different **dialects**, so they pronounce certain words differently. They are called the Lakota, Nakota, or Dakota depending on which dialect they speak.

A Serious Child

When Jumping Badger was young, he was very serious and thoughtful. Because he did not speak until he had thought about his words, he was given the nickname "Slow." As a child, he **participated** in games with the other Hunkpapa boys. These games trained young men to become hunters and warriors. Jumping Badger killed his first buffalo, or

Fast Fact

We know Sitting Bull was born around 1831, but the exact year is uncertain. It could have been any time between 1831 and 1837.

TRIBES OF THE GREAT SIOUX NATION

Dakota	Nakota	Lakota
Waqpekute Wahepton Sisseton Mdewankantonwan	Yankton Yanktonais	Teton Subtribes of the Teton: Oglala Brule Two Kettle Sans Arc Blackfeet Hunkpapa Minneconjou

This shows how the Sioux are grouped. The Yankton and Yanktonais are sometimes considered Dakota groups.

Fast Fact

Counting coup was one of the greatest honors a Lakota warrior could earn. A man counted coup by showing bravery in a fight—for example, risking his life to get close enough to hit an enemy, although the enemy did not have to be killed to make it count.

bison, when he was only 10 years old. At the age of 14, he counted coup on his first enemy. He was no longer a boy after that; he was seen by the Lakota as a man, so he was given a new name: Sitting Bull.

This picture from 1884, drawn by either a Cheyenne or an Arapaho, shows a warrior on a horse counting coup against an enemy.

LAKOTA LIFE

Today, Lakota daily life is generally the same as it is for other Americans. However, life was very different before the **colonizers** arrived. The Lakota were semi-nomadic. This means they would only stay in one place for as long as a bison herd did. Their tipis were easy to put up and take down so they could get on the move quickly.

Lakota children helped their families with chores, but they were also allowed time to play. Many used clay and animal bones to create toys. They also made spinning tops out of bison horns. In some bands, Lakota children enjoyed playing what we call lacrosse.

This picture shows a Lakota camp.

Warrior Groups

After he had proven himself to be a brave warrior, Sitting Bull joined several societies. One of these was called the Kit Fox Warrior Society. Only brave men with good reputations were allowed to join. The members of the Kit Fox Society believed that a person should stay brave and strong at all times, even when they were having a hard time in life. They also believed in being honest and doing good deeds, such as protecting those who could not protect themselves.

Sitting Bull also joined a society called the Strong Heart Society. This was a very **prestigious** society, which only the bravest Lakota warriors were asked to join. The

In some Native American groups, including the Lakota, respected warriors wear feathered war bonnets. Even today, it is disrespectful for anyone who has not earned the bonnet to wear one.

bravest and best in the society were allowed to wear red sashes. Sitting Bull became a sash wearer after he had been in the society for a little while. A short time after that, he became the leader of the whole society.

Becoming a Leader

Sitting Bull's leadership did not end with the Strong Hearts. Around 1868, when he was in his mid-30s, he became a Lakota chief. In this role, he helped the Lakota expand their hunting grounds.

Some Native American groups wanted to work with the U.S. government. They believed it would keep things peaceful and allow them to continue living the way they always had. At the time, they did not realize the government would continually break the promises it was making. Others, including Sitting Bull, spoke out against working with white colonizers.

Fast Fact

Sitting Bull was also a spiritual leader to the Lakota. He had several visions that were later reported to come true. The Lakota greatly admired and respected him.

Prospectors were people who moved to places where gold had been found in the hope of striking it rich. Most did not find any gold, but the towns and mines they built had a big impact on the Native Americans.

HELPING RED CLOUD

Chapter Two

In 1862, a gold rush in what is now the state of Montana caused thousands of white colonizers to move through Lakota hunting land. The government had promised to leave this land alone in a treaty it signed with the Lakota in 1851. However, the government (as well as individual Americans) **violated** that treaty many times.

The Bozeman Trail

A man named John Bozeman created a route called the Bozeman Trail as a shortcut for gold seekers. It cut from the Oregon Trail through Lakota lands in Wyoming and into Montana. The large number of people who traveled the trail every day interfered with the Lakota's ability to hunt. They and other Native American groups, such as the Cheyenne, threatened travelers with violence to get them to stop using the trail, but these threats did not work.

Fast Fact

Red Cloud's War was not the first time Sitting Bull faced off against U.S. soldiers. In 1863, the U.S. Army attacked a group of Lakota in retaliation for the Dakota's 1862 uprising. In 1864, soldiers attacked a Native American trading village. These two events made Sitting Bull swear he would never sign a treaty.

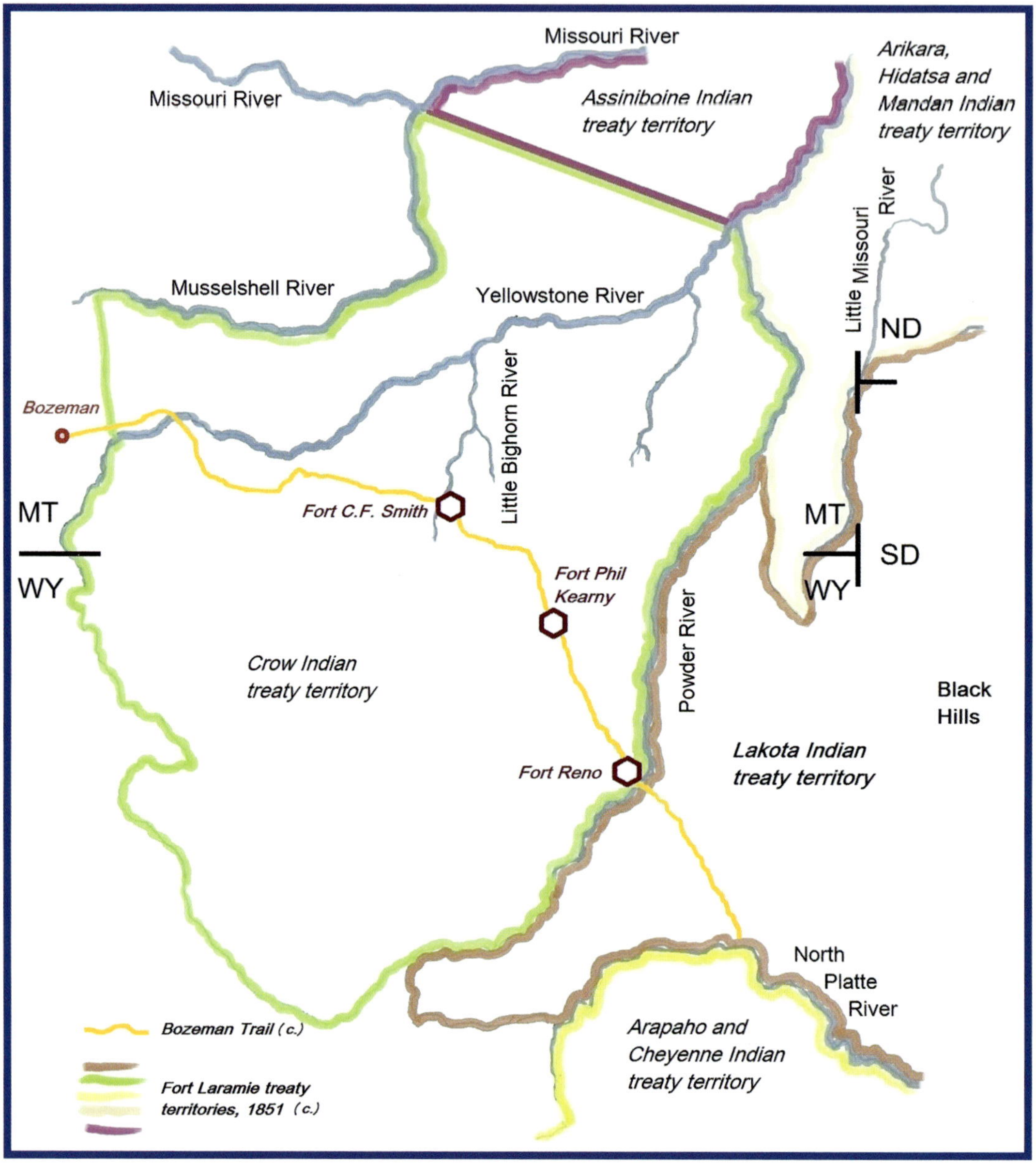

This map shows how the Bozeman Trail cut directly through Lakota land.

The Bozeman Trail had several military forts along its length. The Lakota demanded that the military close the trail and leave the

THE MINNESOTA UPRISING

The U.S. government was dishonest and unfair in many ways in its dealings with Native Americans. For example, treaties the Sioux signed gave the government a lot of Sioux land in exchange for payment. However, the government did not make it a **priority** to pay the Sioux on time.

Since they had given up much of their hunting grounds in treaties, the Sioux people sometimes had trouble finding enough food. They needed the government's money to buy food instead. Because of the late payments, the Dakota were starving in 1862. They realized they could not count on the government's promises, so they decided to drive the white colonizers off their land in Minnesota. The U.S. Army fought back and eventually won.

forts, but the government refused. In 1866, an Oglala Lakota chief named Red Cloud led warriors in a fight against the government. This became known as Red Cloud's War. Sitting Bull joined his people in the fight, attacking several forts.

The Treaty of Fort Laramie

Red Cloud won the war in 1868. He was the only Native American to ever win a war against the U.S. government. That year, the Lakota and the government signed a treaty at Fort Laramie. The treaty said that the United States would stop using the Bozeman Trail. The Lakota had already burned the forts along the trail, and the government agreed not to rebuild and reopen them. The treaty also gave the Lakota some of their land back, including the Black Hills in what is now the state of South Dakota. The government then created the Red Cloud Agency for the Lakota in Nebraska.

Not all of the Lakota were happy with the treaty. Red Cloud's son and Sitting Bull were two of the people who said the Lakota should not sign it. They pointed out that the government was untrustworthy and had broken many treaties in the past.

Fast Fact

Indian agencies, as they were called at the time, were places set up by the government to easily give out supplies to the Native Americans. They were the first **version** of reservations. The Red Cloud Agency was later moved to South Dakota and renamed Pine Ridge Reservation.

Red Cloud was another famous Lakota chief.

The Battle of the Little Bighorn

Sitting Bull turned out to be right. In 1874, gold was discovered in the Black Hills. The government offered to buy that land back from the Lakota. The Lakota refused to sell, but the government still allowed white Americans to move to the Black Hills to look for gold.

Red Cloud and his followers had moved to Pine Ridge Reservation, but Sitting Bull and his followers had not. The U.S. government told Sitting Bull's group that they had until January 31, 1876, to move to Pine Ridge Reservation. If they did not move, the government would consider them hostile, or an enemy, and would attack them.

> **Fast Fact**
>
> Black Elk, an Oglala Lakota who became a famous leader and healer, was about 12 years old when Custer attacked. He was too young to fight, but he was allowed on the battlefield to take clothing and weapons from dead and dying soldiers.

The deadline came and went, and Sitting Bull's people stayed where they were. In June, the army sent Lieutenant Colonel George Custer to the Little Bighorn River to force the Lakota off their land. Custer believed the fight would be easy to win. However, he was mistaken. Custer was killed, and his troops were defeated.

This painting from 1876 shows the Battle of the Little Bighorn.

This picture of Sitting Bull was taken shortly after he surrendered himself to the U.S. Army.

BUFFALO BILL'S WILD WEST

Chapter Three

After the Battle of the Little Bighorn, the U.S. government was more determined than ever to force the Lakota onto reservations—or kill them in the process. The Army also wanted to arrest Sitting Bull for his role in Custer's death. Sitting Bull and his followers realized they would not be safe in the United States. In 1877, they moved to Canada, where they stayed for four years.

Back in the United States

Sitting Bull surrendered to the U.S. Army in 1881. He was held prisoner for two years at Fort Randall in South Dakota, then moved to Standing Rock Reservation on the border between North and South Dakota. Life was hard for him there. He had to adapt to a new way of life, and the white people who ran the reservation did not respect him as a chief. His movements were still controlled by the government, so he had to get permission if he wanted to leave the reservation.

Fast Fact

Sitting Bull's group of Lakota lived in a part of Canada called the Cypress Hills, near Wood Mountain. This is in what is now the province of Saskatchewan.

A law passed in 1851 said Native Americans were not allowed to leave their reservation without permission. This picture from 1880 shows the Standing Rock residents gathered for a census.

A HARSH LIFE

Life in Canada was very hard for Sitting Bull's group of Lakota. There were not many bison for them to hunt. In addition to eating bison meat, the Lakota used bison skin to make things such as clothing and tipis. Without enough bison, they were often hungry and cold. Many got sick, especially during the cold Canadian winters.

Little by little, the group started moving back to the United States. They decided they would rather live on the reservation with the other Lakota than struggle to survive in Canada. By 1881, even the people who were closest to Sitting Bull were ready to return.

On the reservation, the Lakota were learning how to farm so they could support themselves. Sitting Bull was getting old and did not want to farm. Instead, he charged white people money for his picture and **autograph**. He had become famous after the Battle of the Little Bighorn, so many white people wanted to meet him.

Buffalo Bill

In 1883, a man named William Cody started a traveling show he called Buffalo Bill's Wild West. Sitting Bull's fame meant he would be sure to draw a crowd, so in 1885, Cody asked Sitting Bull to join the show. Sitting Bull agreed. He earned $50 per week plus the money he made signing autographs.

Fast Fact

Fifty dollars in 1885 is equal to almost $1,600 in 2024.

Sitting Bull (*left*) and Buffalo Bill Cody (*right*) became friends after Sitting Bull joined the show.

Fast Fact

Buffalo Bill's Wild West claimed to give audiences a window into what living in the American West was like. However, Cody dramatized much of it, giving people false ideas about Native Americans and the "Wild West" that still exist today.

Sitting Bull and other Native Americans who traveled with Buffalo Bill's show used their platform to talk about issues that were important to them. Unfortunately, white audiences were generally more interested in seeing the fake battles, including a reenactment of the Battle of the Little Bighorn, than in listening to what the Native Americans had to say.

Life in the show was often hard for Sitting Bull. Native Americans who traveled with Buffalo Bill were told to act wild and bloodthirsty, which stopped most white people from seeing them as anything other than villains. Crowds would sometimes boo Sitting Bull, and in one city, the brother of a soldier who had died at Little Bighorn attacked him in anger. When the traveling season ended, Sitting Bull went back to Standing Rock. He was not given permission to join the show again the following season.

This picture shows a Ghost Dance event on Pine Ridge Reservation.

GHOST DANCE AND DEATH

Chapter Four

In 1889, a Paiute man named Wovoka started a religion, or faith, called the Ghost Dance. It combined Native American and Christian ideas, and it was both a lifestyle and a religion. In hard times, many people turn to religion to help them feel better. These were certainly hard times for Native Americans, so the movement spread quickly. Sitting Bull was one of the people who was interested in the new religion, although he was not heavily involved.

The White Man's Fear

In 1883, the U.S. government passed a law called the Religious Crimes Code. This outlawed traditional Native American religious practices. When the Ghost Dance started to become popular, government officials became worried.

Fast Fact

Dancing has always been an important part of most Native American religious traditions, or ways.

Many Lakota were involved in the Ghost Dance. Government officials knew Sitting Bull was an important Lakota chief, and they believed he was responsible for the growth of the movement. In the early

The exact person who killed Sitting Bull is unknown. The government never did an investigation. Annie Oakley, a performer in Buffalo Bill's Wild West, remarked that if Sitting Bull had been white, his murderer would have been brought to justice.

WHAT WAS THE GHOST DANCE?

Wovoka said he had seen a vision that white people would one day be gone from North America, leaving Native Americans free to go back to their old ways of life. He said Native Americans could make that happen faster by doing religious dances, not taking drugs or drinking alcohol, working hard, promoting peace, and listening to religious leaders.

Ghost Dance **ceremonies** could last for days. In one four-day ceremony, dancers reported that they had seen visions of the afterworld, where their relatives who had died were living again. The afterworld had plenty of bison and no white people.

Fast Fact

Indian police were policemen who were hired by the government to work on reservations. They enforced the anti-Native American laws the government passed.

morning of December 15, 1890, a group of 40 Indian police went to Sitting Bull's house. They kicked in his door and brought him outside. Details of the account are uncertain, likely because the situation escalated, or grew, so quickly. Sitting Bull was not willing to cooperate with the police. A crowd gathered, and onlookers began yelling at the police to release Sitting Bull. The police began firing their guns, and in only a few moments, Sitting Bull had been shot to death.

Many Native Americans still come to this mass grave at Wounded Knee to pay their respects to the dead.

Fast Fact

The government had asked Buffalo Bill Cody to go to Sitting Bull's house and talk him out of participating in the Ghost Dance. However, he did not arrive until after Sitting Bull had been killed. He was convinced that he could have stopped the murder if he had gotten there earlier, but there is no way to know for sure.

Two weeks after Sitting Bull was killed, the U.S. Army sent 500 soldiers to Wounded Knee Creek, where Ghost Dance ceremonies were often performed. They started shooting the mostly unarmed Native Americans. The horror of this event made Native Americans largely unwilling to continue fighting openly against white Americans.

A Lasting Legacy

Today, Sitting Bull is remembered as one of the most famous and respected Native Americans in history. He worked hard to preserve his people's way of life and keep them safe from the U.S. government. However, more than that, he was a spiritual leader to his people. He offered them advice and leadership when they needed it. His work helped the Lakota keep their traditions alive.

THINK ABOUT IT!

1. Why do you think so many facts about Sitting Bull's early life are uncertain?
2. How could the U.S. government have prevented war with the Lakota, in your opinion?
3. Why do you think Buffalo Bill told the Native Americans in his show to act bloodthirsty?
4. Why do you think the government outlawed Native American religious practices?

TIMELINE

Sitting Bull's Life	World Events
1831 Sitting Bull is born.	**1831** Charles Darwin sets sail on the HMS *Beagle*.
	1851 The *New York Times* is founded.
	1867 The U.S. government buys Alaska from Russia.
1868 Sitting Bull becomes a Lakota chief.	
	1871 Rome becomes the capital of Italy.
1876 Battle of the Little Bighorn	
1877–1881 Sitting Bull lives in Canada to escape the U.S. government.	
	1882 Congress passes the Chinese Exclusion Act, which bans all immigration from China.
1885 He tours with Buffalo Bill's Wild West.	
	1888 Serial killer Jack the Ripper is on the loose in London, England.
1890 Sitting Bull dies.	

GLOSSARY

autograph: A person's handwritten signature.

census: A count of the population of a certain area.

ceremony: A formal act or series of acts performed in a certain way.

colonizer: A person who moves to another country to live on land that was taken from a Native group.

dialect: A variety of a language that is different in certain areas.

participate: To take part in something.

prestigious: Having importance in the eyes of other people.

priority: A condition of being given attention first.

retaliate: To get back at someone for a real or perceived injury or injustice.

version: A form or variant of something.

violate: To fail to keep or observe.

FIND OUT MORE

Books

Beason, Jimmy. *Native Americans in History: A History Book for Kids*. Emeryville, CA: Rockridge Press, 2021.

Bird, F. A. *Lakota*. Minneapolis, MN: Checkerboard Library, 2022.

Katirgis, Jane, and Chris Hayhurst. *Meet Sitting Bull, Lakota Chief*. New York, NY: Enslow Publishing, 2020.

Websites

Ducksters: Sitting Bull
www.ducksters.com/history/native_americans/sitting_bull.php
Learn more about Sitting Bull's life.

Kiddle: Sitting Bull Facts for Kids
kids.kiddle.co/Sitting_Bull
Read about Sitting Bull's role in the fights between the Lakota and the U.S. government.

Travel South Dakota: Native Americans in South Dakota
www.travelsouthdakota.com/kids-online-lessons/native-americans-south-dakota
This website gives a short overview of Lakota culture and includes activities kids can do at home.

INDEX